DROPPING IN ON matisse

By Pamela Geiger Stephens
Illustrations by Don Wass

CrystalProductions
Aspen, Colorado   Glenview, Illinois

Library of Congress Cataloging-in-Publication Data

Stephens, Pamela Geiger.
  Dropping in on Matisse / by Pamela Geiger Stephens ;
illustrations by Don Wass.— 1st ed.
      p. cm.
  ISBN 1-56290-322-5
  1. Matisse, Henri, 1869-1954—Juvenile literature. 2. Art
appreciation—Juvenile literature. I. Wass, Don, 1967- II. Title.
  ND553.M37S74 2004
  759.4—dc22
                              2004009328

ISBN 1-56290-322-5

Printed in Hong Kong

Hello there. My name is Puffer. Today I am on my way to visit the famous French artist, Henri Matisse. Mister Matisse lives in the South of France near the Mediterranean Sea.

Would you like to come along?

My map shows that we are near Mister Matisse's home.

Yikes! I forgot that I am flying!

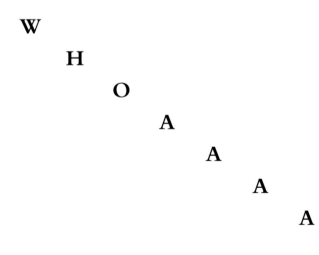

Flap! Flap! Flap!

Look out below!!!!

Flutter! Flutter! Flutter! Flap!

Thump! Bump! Crash!

Oomph!

Mister Matisse hurries to the balcony to investigate the noise.

"Hello? What's this? What's that racket?" he asked.

"Oh, hello, Mister Matisse. I am Puffer. You were expecting me, sir. I am here to talk to you about your artwork."

"Yes, yes! Puffer, the interviewer," laughed Mister Matisse. "I am glad to meet you, but I didn't expect you to fall from the sky."

"I've never been very good at landings."

"Perhaps learning to land is a little like learning to make art. You have to practice and practice and practice to become good at it."

"I think you are very right."

Mister Matisse invites Puffer into his studio. The studio is filled with all sorts of artwork. Bits of colored paper litter the floor.

"There is so much artwork in your studio, Mister Matisse! I hardly know where to begin looking."

"Perhaps you would like to see one of my first well-known paintings," suggested Mister Matisse. "But first I must warn you that after this painting was in an art show, I was called a *wild beast*."

"A wild beast? Why would an artist be called such a thing?"

"Let's look at the painting and you can figure that out for yourself," said Mister Matisse.

"That would be splendid!"

"The title of this painting is *Woman with the Hat*. It is a portrait of my wife," said Mister Matisse as he pointed to a colorful painting on the wall.

"*Woman with the Hat* must have been quite a surprise to the people who first saw the painting."

"Surprise indeed! People did not expect to see splotches of blue, yellow, green, and pink on Madame Matisse's face!" exclaimed Mister Matisse. "Seeing flat shapes instead of little details was a surprise as well. Soon I was called a *fauve*."

"Fauve?"

"That's a French word that means *wild beast*," explained Mister Matisse.

"Are the bright colors and flat shapes why you were called a wild beast?"

"That is one story," chuckled Mister Matisse. "Another story is that I wore a big, furry coat to an art show and people thought I looked like a wild beast!"

"This makes me very curious, Mister Matisse. Would you tell me about your life now?"

"With pleasure," Mister Matisse said. "Let's go sit by the window."

"I was born on New Year's Eve in 1869 in a small town in Northern France," Mister Matisse said. "My parents owned a general store. They hoped that one day I would take over the family business, but working in the store did not interest me.

"I wanted to become a lawyer so I went away to law school," Mister Matisse continued. "After I finished college, I returned home and went to work in a law office.

"I had not been home too long when I became very sick. Staying in bed was very boring until my mother brought some art supplies to me. Then I began to draw and draw and draw. Before too long, I knew that I wanted to be an artist.

"My father was unhappy with my idea, but he agreed to send me to art school in Paris anyway," added Mister Matisse. "In Paris I met many other artists, visited art museums, and worked very hard to become a successful artist. This was when I became known as a wild beast.

"Would you like to see another painting from that time, Puffer?" Mister Matisse asked.

"Yes, I would, Mister Matisse!"

Mister Matisse points to another colorful painting on the studio wall.

"I call this painting *View of Collioure*," said Mister Matisse. "This painting was made at about the same time as *Woman with the Hat*. Do you see how both paintings are the same?"

"Yes, I do! Both paintings are made with unusual colors."

"You are a good art observer, Puffer," Mister Matisse responded. "When I paint with blue, it is not always the sky. When I paint with green, it is not always the grass."

"I also see simple, flat shapes without many details."

"Now you know why this kind of artwork caused such a fuss," added Mister Matisse. "People were used to seeing pictures that looked real. Not too many people understood my new art ideas."

"I am glad that there were *some* people who understood your artwork, Mister Matisse."

As Puffer writes notes about the artwork, Mister Matisse continues to talk.

"*Woman with the Hat* and *View of Collioure* helped to changed the way that everyone looked at art. These two paintings helped me to become known as a Father of Modern Art," Mister Matisse said proudly.

"What is modern art, Mister Matisse?"

"Modern art," explained Mister Matisse, "is about trying new ideas and changing the ways that art can be made. Modern art helps us to think and see ideas in different ways."

"Maybe I need to see some more examples to better understand. May I please see another of your paintings?"

"But of course," Mister Matisse replied. "Shall we look at a painting that I call *Goldfish*?"

"Please, let's do that."

"Do you see harmony in *Goldfish*?" asked Mister Matisse.

"Harmony? Isn't that a word used in music?"

"Harmony is a word that is used in art *and* music," explained Mister Matisse. "Harmony in art is the way that all the parts of a picture fit together. To find the harmony, all you have to do is figure out how all of the parts fit together. For example, look at all the round shapes in *Goldfish*."

"Round shapes are repeated everywhere," exclaimed Puffer. There is a round table, a round jar, and round leaves. Even the eyes of the goldfish are round!"

"There is harmony in the color, too," said Mister Matisse. "If you look closely, you will see how everything seems tied together with green, pink, and black."

"The colors and shapes in *Goldfish* are very restful, Mister Matisse."

"That was my idea," Mister Matisse smiled. "To me, a painting should be as comfortable as an old chair."

"I was wondering, Mister Matisse, have you made other kinds of artwork besides paintings?"

"Oh, my, yes!" exclaimed Mister Matisse. "After I moved here, I tried all sorts of art ideas and materials. I designed sets and costumes for a ballet. Then I learned about printmaking and how to make sculpture. I drew pictures for poems and a book. I created a mural. But as always, I painted and painted and painted."

"You were very busy then!"

"I am still busy," said Mister Matisse. "Some days I make art while I sit in bed, just like when I was a young man. Many of my paintings show the inside of my studio. Others show what is just outside my window."

"May we see one of those paintings?"

"I would be delighted to show one to you," Mister Matisse replied.

"This is *Interior with Egyptian Curtain*," said Mister Matisse as he points to a nearby painting. "What do you see in this artwork?"

"I see a large glass window with a black curtain hanging down one side. A red, yellow, green, and white pattern covers the curtain. Below the window is a small table. A bowl of round fruit sits on the table. Outside is a palm tree that reminds me of exploding fireworks."

"Excellent!" exclaimed Mister Matisse. "You have found the most important objects in the painting. Do you see how the lines and colors are used in this painting?"

"The lines guide my eyes around the picture so that I see the most important objects. There are only a few colors. Having black next to the other colors makes them seem very bright."

"Exactly!" said Mister Matisse. "What about the space in the painting?"

"The space is a little mysterious to me. I cannot tell how far away any of the objects are."

Mister Matisse smiled and then asked, "All good artwork should have a little mystery, don't you think?"

As Mister Matisse and Puffer sit on the balcony, they see unusual sailboats in the distance.

"There is my old friend Pablo Picasso enjoying a sunny day," Mister Matisse said. "When we were young, Pablo and I did not agree about much of anything! Nowadays we are good friends who share our ideas and artwork.

"Pablo thinks that I am the only artist in the whole world whose work is as good as his," Mister Matisse proudly added.

"What an interesting friend you have, Mister Matisse!"

"I certainly agree," replied Mister Matisse. "Are you ready to see some more artwork?"

"Yes, please."

Mister Matisse shows Puffer a special work of art that is different from anything Puffer had ever seen.

The title of this work of art is *Les Codomas*," said Mister Matisse "It is what I call a paper cutout."

"A paper cutout? What is that?"

"Paper cutouts are my own art invention," Mister Matisse replied. "I cut shapes from painted paper and then carefully paste the shapes to a background."

"I see that every color, line, and shape in *Les Codomas* is in just the right place, Mister Matisse."

"I plan each paper cutout as carefully as my paintings," Mister Matisse explained. "Do you see that *Les Codomas* is about the circus?"

"Yes, I do! The two yellow shapes are acrobats who leap from their trapeze bars. Below them is a safety net made from black squares and rectangles."

"You are a good art observer, my friend!" exclaimed Mister Matisse. "I have made many paper cutouts. Would you like to see another?"

"I would!"

"Before I tell you the title of this paper cutout, I will let you describe what you see," said Mister Matisse.

"Hmmm. There are three main shapes. The three main shapes, I think, are people. The green shape pounds on a drum, the black shape strums a guitar, and the white shape dances."

"What do you think all of this means?" asked Mister Matisse.

"It seems to be a celebration of some sort. Would you please tell me the title now?"

"It is called *The Sadness of the King* and it is a celebration. The king is celebrating his long life. Around him are the things he has loved," replied Mister Matisse.

"Could the king be you, Mister Matisse?"

"Some people seem to think so," Mister Matisse answered.

"Mister Matisse, you have shown us that trying new art ideas can be difficult. But, because you never gave up, you became a successful artist."

"Remember, making good art takes time and practice," said Mister Matisse.

"Oh, my goodness! Speaking of time, it is time to go! Thank you for showing us your artwork, Mister Matisse!"

"You are very welcome," replied Mister Matisse as he watched his new friend prepare to fly away.

"Au revoir! Good-bye!"

I hope you had fun dropping in on Henri Matisse. Learning about artists and their artwork helps us to understand our world a little better.

You can find Mister Matisse's artwork in museums all over the world. Maybe one day you will see one his paintings or sculptures or even a paper cutout.

Until I see you again ...au revoir! Good-bye!

GLOSSARY

Au revoir A French phrase that means "good-bye"

Elements of Art The basic components of art: color, line, shape, form, texture, value, and space

Fauve (Fohv) A French word that means "wild beast"

Harmony A principle of design that refers to the way the elements of art interrelate in a composition

Henri Matisse French artist who lived from 1869-1954

Modern Art Up-to-date; breaking with art traditions of the past

Pablo Picasso Spanish artist who lived from 1881-1973

Painting Works of art created with paint that has been applied to a surface

Paper cutout A kind of art product developed by Matisse wherein paper was coated with gouache, a design was cut from the prepared paper, and the design was applied to another ground

Woman with the Hat (Femme au chapeau), 1905
Oil on canvas, 31¾ x 23½ in. (80.65 x 59.69 cm)
San Francisco Museum of Modern Art, Bequest of Elise S. Haas. © 2004 Succession H. Matisse, Paris / Artists Rights Society (ARS), New York

Roofs of Collioure (View of Collioure), c. 1905
Oil on canvas, 23¼ x 28½ in. (59 x 73 cm)
Hermitage St. Petersburg, Russia / Bridgeman Art Library © 2004 Succession H. Matisse, Paris / Artists Rights Society (ARS), New York

Goldfish, 1911
Oil on canvas, 57⅞ x 35⅝ in. (145 x 95 cm)
© 2004 Succession H. Matisse, Paris / Artists Rights Society (ARS), New York. Pushkin Museum, Moscow, Russia / Bridgeman Art Library

Interior with Egyptian Curtain, 1948
Oil on canvas, 45¾ x 35⅛ in. (116.2 x 89.2 cm)
Phillips Collection, Washington, DC / Giraudon-Bridgeman Art Library. © 2004 Succession H. Matisse, Paris / Artists Rights Society (ARS), New York

Les Codomas from the *Jazz* series, 1947
Gouache on cut-and-pasted paper, 16¾ x 25¾ in. (42.5 x 65.5 cm). © 2004 Succession H. Matisse, Paris / Artists Rights Society (ARS), New York. CNAC / MNAM / Dist. Réunion des Mus es Nationaux / Art Resource, NY Musée National d'Art Moderne, Centre Georges Pompidou, Paris, France

Sadness of the King (Tristesse du Roi), 1952
Gouache-painted cut papers mounted on canvas, 115 x 155⅞ in. © 2004 Succession H. Matisse, Paris / Artists Rights Society (ARS), New York. Copyright Erich Lessing / Art Resource, NY. Musée National d'Art Moderne, Centre Georges Pompidou, Paris, France